MW01617951

Publisher: 3dots Publishing

www.dadisworld.com

Creative & Illustrations: Yael Eshet
Thoughts & Comments: Rachel Stein
Graphic Execution: Liron Avrami

Life Lessons from Dad

A Keepsake Journal

A one-of-a-kind journal of life lessons and advice –

WRITTEN BY DAD!

HOW TO USE THIS JOURNAL

52 significant life lessons from Dad to child are collected in this book.

1. *These life lessons capture the experience, knowledge, and wisdom a father gathers over the years, which he wants to pass on to his family.*
2. *Covering everything from love and family to technology and happiness, this thoughtful journal addresses all the important things in life.*
3. *Each topic has plenty of space for you to create a meaningful keepsake and share everything you've learned about life with your children.*
4. *Make the life lessons uniquely yours by expressing them in your own words. Let your voice shine—be emotional, humorous, realistic—just be yourself!*

Additional pages are included to help your children get to know you, Dad:

1. *All About Dad: write down your life goals, values, achievements, and memories so your family can learn more about you!*
2. *Trace your handprint so your loved ones can connect with you anytime!*
3. *Inspire your children by creating a complete roadmap for life based on your worldview, experiences, and insights!*

 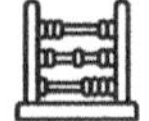            

Hand in Hand

①

Trace Dad's hand.

②

Trace kids' or other family members' hands inside of dad's hand.

Visit our website

www.dadisworld.com

IF YOU WANT MORE

Scan to Visit Store

All About Dad

What Makes Me Proud

The things that fill me with pride, from my achievements to the people I love.

All About Dad

The Things I Love Most

A collection of the people, places, and things that bring me the greatest joy.

All About Dad

My Favorite Family Traditions

Special family traditions that mean a lot to me and bring us closer together.

All About Dad

My Values

The core beliefs and principles that guide my decisions and shape who I am.

All About Dad

My Best Childhood Memories

A few of my most memorable experiences and memories as a kid.

All About Dad

What I've Learned as a Parent

Reflections on the joys and challenges of parenthood and how being a dad has changed me.

All About Dad

My Life Goals

The dreams and aspirations I've set for myself, and the journey I'm on to achieve them.

All About Dad

My Biggest Achievements

The moments and accomplishments I'm most proud of and what they mean to me.

CONTENTS

ALL ABOUT DAD

WISDOM, THOUGHTS AND TIPS:

Dad's Life Advice About

OUR WORLD

Wisdom, Thoughts and Tips:

Dad's Life Advice About

WINNING

WISDOM, THOUGHTS AND TIPS:

Dad's Life Advice About

TRAVEL

WISDOM, THOUGHTS AND TIPS:

Dad's Life Advice About

TOYS

Wisdom, thoughts and tips:

Dad's Life Advice About

TIME

WISDOM, THOUGHTS AND TIPS:

Dad's Life Advice About

TECHNOLOGY

WISDOM, THOUGHTS AND TIPS:

Dad's Life Advice About

SUPERHEROS

Wisdom, thoughts and tips:

Dad's Life Advice About

SUCCESS

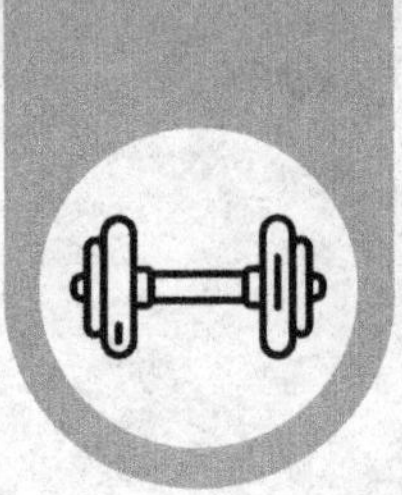

Wisdom, thoughts and tips:

Dad's Life Advice About

WISDOM, THOUGHTS AND TIPS:

Dad's Life Advice About

SPORTS

WISDOM, THOUGHTS AND TIPS:

Dad's Life Advice About

SLEEP

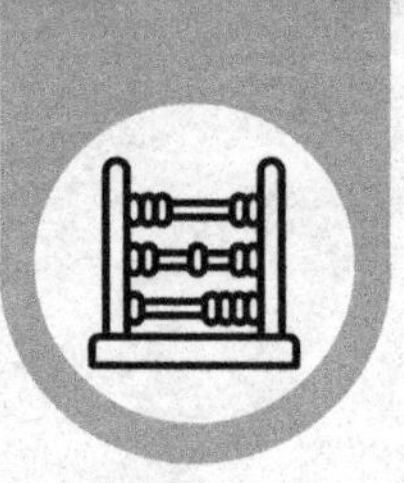

WISDOM, THOUGHTS AND TIPS:

Dad's Life Advice About

SCHOOL

WISDOM, THOUGHTS AND TIPS:

Dad's Life Advice About

ROLE MODELS

WISDOM, THOUGHTS AND TIPS:

Dad's Life Advice About

PROGRESS

WISDOM, THOUGHTS AND TIPS:

Dad's Life Advice About

POPULARITY

WISDOM, THOUGHTS AND TIPS:

Dad's Life Advice About

PETS

WISDOM, THOUGHTS AND TIPS:

Dad's Life Advice About

OUTDOORS

Wisdom, thoughts and tips:

Dad's Life Advice About

MUSIC

WISDOM, THOUGHTS AND TIPS:

Dad's Life Advice About

MOVIES

Wisdom, thoughts and tips:

Dad's Life Advice About

MOTIVATION

WISDOM, THOUGHTS AND TIPS:

Dad's Life Advice About

MONEY

WISDOM, THOUGHTS AND TIPS:

Dad's Life Advice About

MEMORIES

WISDOM, THOUGHTS AND TIPS:

Dad's Life Advice About

LUCK

WISDOM, THOUGHTS AND TIPS:

Dad's Life Advice About

LOVE

WISDOM, THOUGHTS AND TIPS:

Dad's Life Advice About

KNOWLEDGE

Wisdom, thoughts and tips:

Dad's Life Advice About
KINDNESS

WISDOM, THOUGHTS AND TIPS:

Dad's Life Advice About

JUSTICE

WISDOM, THOUGHTS AND TIPS:

Dad's Life Advice About

HUMOR

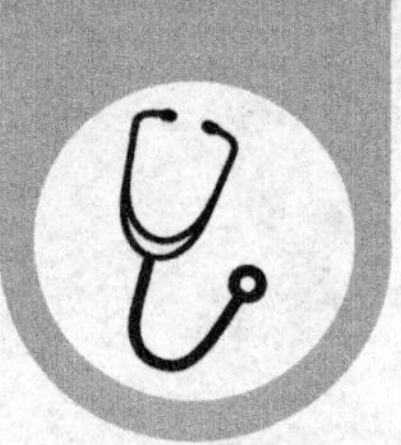

WISDOM, THOUGHTS AND TIPS:

Dad's Life Advice About

HEALTH

Wisdom, Thoughts and Tips:

Dad's Life Advice About

HAPPINESS

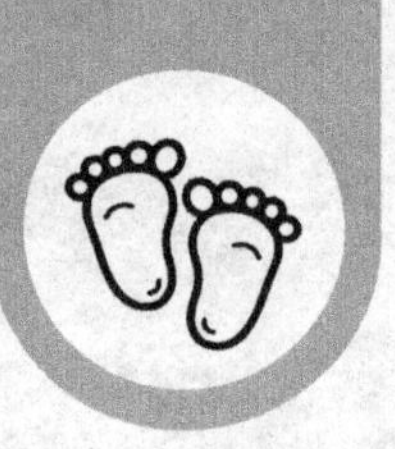

WISDOM, THOUGHTS AND TIPS:

Dad's Life Advice About

GROWING UP

Wisdom, thoughts and tips:

Dad's Life Advice About

GOOD & BAD

Wisdom, thoughts and tips:

Dad's Life Advice About

THE FUTURE

WISDOM, THOUGHTS AND TIPS:

Dad's Life Advice About

FUN

Wisdom, thoughts and tips:

Dad's Life Advice About

FRIENDS

WISDOM, THOUGHTS AND TIPS:

Dad's Life Advice About

FOOD

WISDOM, THOUGHTS AND TIPS:

Dad's Life Advice About

FIGHTING

WISDOM, THOUGHTS AND TIPS:

Dad's Life Advice About

FEAR

WISDOM, THOUGHTS AND TIPS:

Dad's Life Advice About

FAMILY

Wisdom, thoughts and tips:

Dad's Life Advice About

FAITH

WISDOM, THOUGHTS AND TIPS:

Dad's Life Advice About

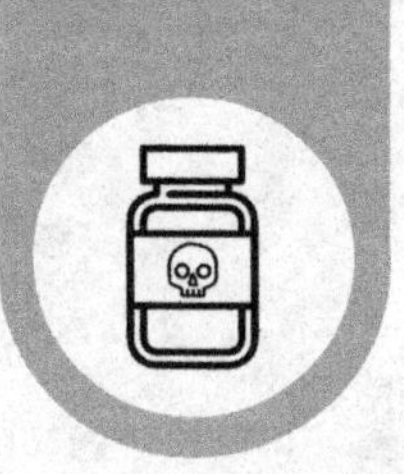

Wisdom, thoughts and tips:

Dad's Life Advice About
DRUGS

WISDOM, THOUGHTS AND TIPS:

Dad's Life Advice About

DREAMS

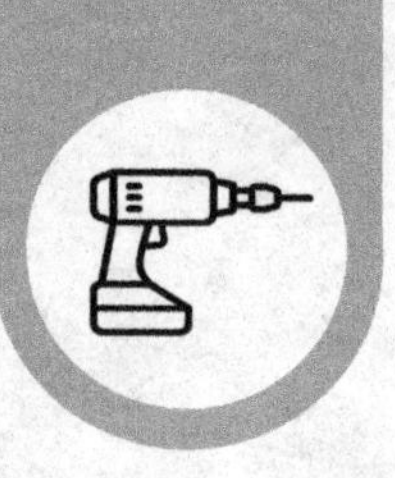

WISDOM, THOUGHTS AND TIPS:

Dad's Life Advice About

DIY

WISDOM, THOUGHTS AND TIPS:

Dad's Life Advice About

DATING

Wisdom, thoughts and tips:

Dad's Life Advice About

CULTURE

WISDOM, THOUGHTS AND TIPS:

Dad's Life Advice About

WISDOM, THOUGHTS AND TIPS:

Dad's Life Advice About

CONFIDENCE

Wisdom, thoughts and tips:

Dad's Life Advice About

COMMUNITY

WISDOM, THOUGHTS AND TIPS:

Dad's Life Advice About

CHOICES

WISDOM, THOUGHTS AND TIPS:

Dad's Life Advice About

CHALLENGES

Wisdom, Thoughts and Tips:

Dad's Life Advice About

CAREER

CONTENTS

DAD'S LIFE ADVICE

Trace your hand here